# CHRISTMAS HANDBOOK

by Leone Castell Anderson
Dotti Hannum
Patricia Stone Martin
Jane Belk Moncure
and others

illustrated by Gwen Connelly

THE CHILD'S WORLD

ELGIN, ILLINOIS 60120

EDITOR: Diane Dow Suire

Distributed by Childrens Press, 1224 West Van Buren Street, Chicago, Illinois 60607.

**Library of Congress Cataloging in Publication Data**

Main entry under title:

Christmas handbook.

1. Creative activities and seat work.    2. Christmas.
3. Educational games.    4. Christmas decorations.
5. Handicraft.    I. Hannum, Dotti.
LB1537.C552   1984              790.1'922              83-26149
ISBN 0-89565-268-4

1 2 3 4 5 6 7 8 9 10 11 12 R 89 88 87 86 85 84

# CHRISTMAS
# HANDBOOK

# USING THIS HANDBOOK

*(For teachers of students in grades K-3)*

You can use the most anticipated month of the year — December — to increase your students' interest in learning via the potpourri of activities found in this handbook.

You'll find great imagination-stretcher ideas in language arts and math. You'll discover information on how Christmas customs and traditions came to be. In addition, there are decorations to brighten your classroom, happy songs to sing, gifts to make and give, games to play, stories to read, poems to share, a fun-filled play to perform, and other value-affirming activities.

Treat your students to some of the holiday activities found in this book . . . and watch the magic happen!

# CONTENTS

Using this Handbook . . . . . . . . . . . . . . .     4

Table of Contents . . . . . . . . . . . . . . . . .     5

Holiday History . . . . . . . . . . . . . . . . . .     9

Before the Rush (Preparation Ideas)  . . . .    10

## CHRISTMAS AROUND THE ROOM

Room Decorations

- Tissue Paper Wreath . . . . . . . . . . . . . . . . . . . . .    14
- Gingerbread Boys and Girls . . . . . . . . . . . . . . . .    15
- Doorknob Decoration . . . . . . . . . . . . . . . . . . . .    16
- Paper Roll Santa . . . . . . . . . . . . . . . . . . . . . . . .    17
- Star Santa . . . . . . . . . . . . . . . . . . . . . . . . . . . . .    18
- Christmas Stockings . . . . . . . . . . . . . . . . . . . . .    19
- Sparkle Ball . . . . . . . . . . . . . . . . . . . . . . . . . . . .    20
- Pom-pom Wreaths . . . . . . . . . . . . . . . . . . . . . .    21

Tree Trims from Nature

- Tree Chains . . . . . . . . . . . . . . . . . . . . . . . . . . . .    22
- Acorn Bells . . . . . . . . . . . . . . . . . . . . . . . . . . . . .    22
- Walnut Elves and Santas . . . . . . . . . . . . . . . . . .    23
- Seed Stars . . . . . . . . . . . . . . . . . . . . . . . . . . . . .    23
- A Natural Tree . . . . . . . . . . . . . . . . . . . . . . . . . .    24
- Milkweed Pets . . . . . . . . . . . . . . . . . . . . . . . . . .    25
- Pinecone People . . . . . . . . . . . . . . . . . . . . . . . .    25

Bulletin Board Ideas

- Christmas Sights . . . . . . . . . . . . . . . . . . . . . . . .    26
- Christmas Smells . . . . . . . . . . . . . . . . . . . . . . . .    27
- Christmas Colors . . . . . . . . . . . . . . . . . . . . . . . .    28
- Christmas Sounds . . . . . . . . . . . . . . . . . . . . . . .    28
- Christmas Animals on Parade . . . . . . . . . . . . . . .    30

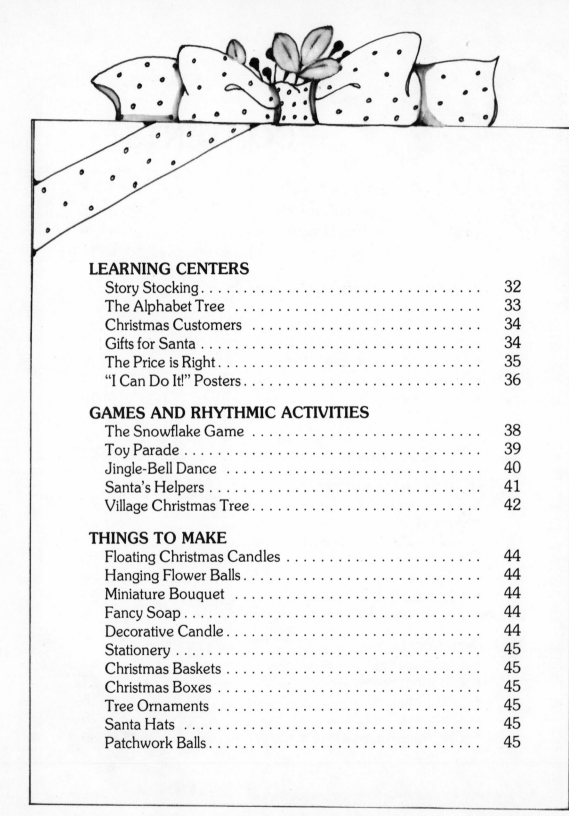

## LEARNING CENTERS

Story Stocking . . . . . . . . . . . . . . . . . . . . . . . . . . . 32
The Alphabet Tree . . . . . . . . . . . . . . . . . . . . . . . . 33
Christmas Customers . . . . . . . . . . . . . . . . . . . . . 34
Gifts for Santa . . . . . . . . . . . . . . . . . . . . . . . . . . . 34
The Price is Right . . . . . . . . . . . . . . . . . . . . . . . . 35
"I Can Do It!" Posters . . . . . . . . . . . . . . . . . . . . . 36

## GAMES AND RHYTHMIC ACTIVITIES

The Snowflake Game . . . . . . . . . . . . . . . . . . . . . 38
Toy Parade . . . . . . . . . . . . . . . . . . . . . . . . . . . . . 39
Jingle-Bell Dance . . . . . . . . . . . . . . . . . . . . . . . . 40
Santa's Helpers . . . . . . . . . . . . . . . . . . . . . . . . . 41
Village Christmas Tree . . . . . . . . . . . . . . . . . . . . 42

## THINGS TO MAKE

Floating Christmas Candles . . . . . . . . . . . . . . . . 44
Hanging Flower Balls . . . . . . . . . . . . . . . . . . . . . 44
Miniature Bouquet . . . . . . . . . . . . . . . . . . . . . . . 44
Fancy Soap . . . . . . . . . . . . . . . . . . . . . . . . . . . . . 44
Decorative Candle . . . . . . . . . . . . . . . . . . . . . . . 44
Stationery . . . . . . . . . . . . . . . . . . . . . . . . . . . . . . 45
Christmas Baskets . . . . . . . . . . . . . . . . . . . . . . . 45
Christmas Boxes . . . . . . . . . . . . . . . . . . . . . . . . 45
Tree Ornaments . . . . . . . . . . . . . . . . . . . . . . . . . 45
Santa Hats . . . . . . . . . . . . . . . . . . . . . . . . . . . . . 45
Patchwork Balls . . . . . . . . . . . . . . . . . . . . . . . . . 45

Crèche . . . . . . . . . . . . . . . . . . . . . . . 46
Old-Fashioned Ornaments . . . . . . . . . . . . . . . . . . . 47
Christmas Vase . . . . . . . . . . . . . . . . . . . . . . . . . 48
Dipping Candles . . . . . . . . . . . . . . . . . . . . . . . . 49
Keepsake Christmas Ornaments . . . . . . . . . . . . . . . 50

## MUSIC AND DRAMA

"Share Your Love" (Song) . . . . . . . . . . . . . . . . . 52
"I Can Be a Christmas Star" (Song) . . . . . . . . . . . . 52
"Snowflakes" (Song) . . . . . . . . . . . . . . . . . . . . . 53
"Ding! Dong! Little Bell" (Song) . . . . . . . . . . . . . . 54
"Christmas Magic" (Play) . . . . . . . . . . . . . . . . . . 55
"The Magic Word for Christmas" (Song) . . . . . . . . . . 60

## CUSTOMS AND TRADITIONS

The Christmas Tree . . . . . . . . . . . . . . . . . . . . . 64
Evergreens . . . . . . . . . . . . . . . . . . . . . . . . . . 65
The Yule Log . . . . . . . . . . . . . . . . . . . . . . . . . 66
Lights . . . . . . . . . . . . . . . . . . . . . . . . . . . . . 66
Christmas Carols . . . . . . . . . . . . . . . . . . . . . . . 67
The Crèche . . . . . . . . . . . . . . . . . . . . . . . . . . 68
Bells . . . . . . . . . . . . . . . . . . . . . . . . . . . . . . 68
Stockings . . . . . . . . . . . . . . . . . . . . . . . . . . . 69
Gifts . . . . . . . . . . . . . . . . . . . . . . . . . . . . . . 70
Cards . . . . . . . . . . . . . . . . . . . . . . . . . . . . . 70
Foods . . . . . . . . . . . . . . . . . . . . . . . . . . . . . 71

## CHRISTMAS AROUND THE WORLD . . . . . . . . . . . . 73

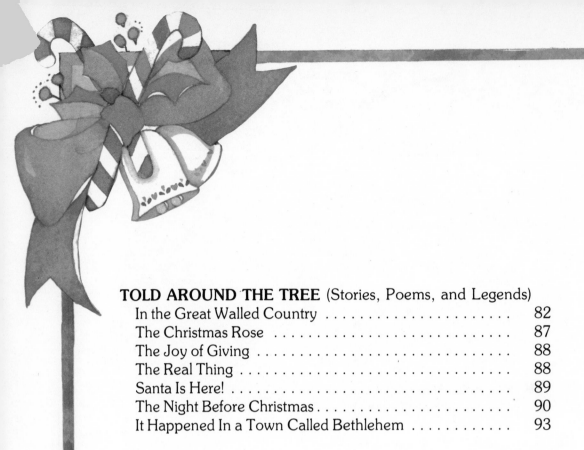

## TOLD AROUND THE TREE (Stories, Poems, and Legends)

In the Great Walled Country . . . . . . . . . . . . . . . . . . . . . . 82

The Christmas Rose . . . . . . . . . . . . . . . . . . . . . . . 87

The Joy of Giving . . . . . . . . . . . . . . . . . . . . . . . . . . 88

The Real Thing . . . . . . . . . . . . . . . . . . . . . . . . . . . 88

Santa Is Here! . . . . . . . . . . . . . . . . . . . . . . . . . . . 89

The Night Before Christmas . . . . . . . . . . . . . . . . . . . . . 90

It Happened In a Town Called Bethlehem . . . . . . . . . . . 93

# HOLIDAY HISTORY

How did Christmas begin? It began when people started celebrating the birthday of Jesus of Nazareth.

The story in the Bible tells of His birth. We read that a ruling was made by Caesar Augustus, the Roman emperor. He said everyone must go to his own city to be taxed. So Joseph took Mary to Bethlehem. When they arrived, the city was so crowded, there was no place for them to stay but in a stable. Mary's baby was born there, and the baby's first bed was a manger. The baby was a special child, the Bible tells us. Angels announced His birth. Shepherds came to worship Him. And Wise-men, following a star, came bringing gifts to the child.

When was Jesus born? No one really knows, for exact records were not kept then. Later, when the church fathers wanted to celebrate Jesus' birth, they chose December 25. They probably made the choice because the Roman people already had a celebration around that time of year. It was to honor a pagan god called Saturnus. The Romans celebrated their holiday "Saturna-lia" by eating, singing, being merry, and giving gifts to each other. These ways were adopted by the Christians to celebrate Christmas. (Of course, Christians also give gifts because of the gifts brought by the Wise-men.)

Where did we get the word, "Christmas"? The use of this word came about years ago in the country of England. During an early type of celebration, people were asked to leave gifts in church. After the service, the gifts were given to the needy by the parish priest. This service came to be known as Christ's Mass, or Christmas for short.

Christmas began many hundreds of years ago, and the spirit of Christmas is still alive. It's alive in all the customs and traditions we follow. And we keep the spirit of Christmas alive by sharing love, warmth, and kindness.

# BEFORE THE RUSH

## (Preparation Ideas)

Here are some ideas to help you celebrate the Christmas season in a variety of ways.

• Read a Christmas classic to your pupils during the month of December. Davie's "Miracle on 34th Street," Alden's "In The Great Walled Country," and Bigson's "Christmas Through a Knothole," are a few classics that depict some lasting themes of the season. See the "Told Around the Tree" section in this book or consult your local library for these and other stories.

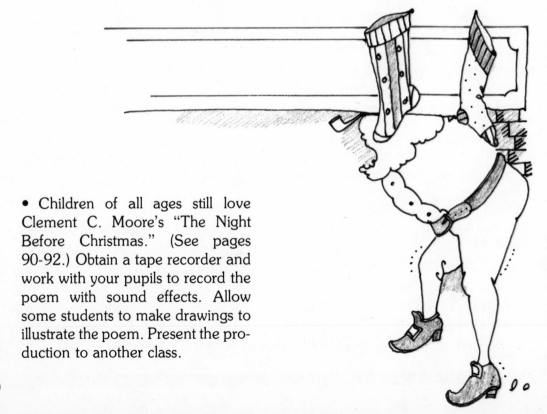

• Children of all ages still love Clement C. Moore's "The Night Before Christmas." (See pages 90-92.) Obtain a tape recorder and work with your pupils to record the poem with sound effects. Allow some students to make drawings to illustrate the poem. Present the production to another class.

• Help your pupils create a lasting reminder of the Christmas season. Let them begin their own scrapbooks the first week of December. They may add drawings, Christmas handouts, party souvenirs, cards and invitations, etc.

• Plan to remember the animals during this season. Invite pupils to bring in bread crumbs, nuts, bird seed, and carrots. Take pupils on a winter outdoor walk where they can leave their "gifts" for our furry and feathered friends.

• Get permission to decorate a live tree on school property. Then invite the whole school to a "lighting ceremony." Let your class lead the audience in a festive carol sing. See pages 52-54, and 60 for some new songs.

- Plan a songfest. Let the pupils sing to school personnel who deserve appreciation—the principal, school nurse, cooks, custo- dians, hall monitors, secretaries, bus drivers, teacher aides, etc. Use some of your pupils' favorite songs.

- Spread the Christmas cheer! Make decorations for windows in the rooms of hospital patients. Let the pupils deliver the decorations if possible. See pages 14-21 for decoration ideas.

- Utilize discarded materials for special Christmas craft gifts. Cut out figures from old Christmas cards to make mobiles. Use a shoe box to make a Christmas scene. Let pupils mount pictures from Christmas cards on craft sticks to use as puppets for skits they create. See pages 44-50 for more craft ideas.

# CHRISTMAS AROUND THE ROOM

# ROOM DECORATIONS
*by Dotti Hannum and others*

Children enjoy the fun of decorating at Christmas. Why not let them make their classroom look merry and bright by creating some of the following fun decorations!

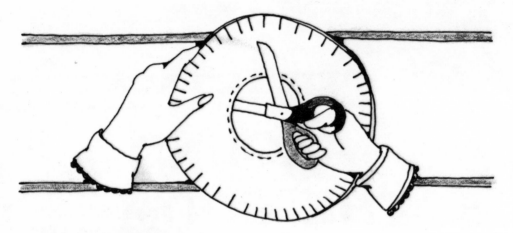

## TISSUE PAPER WREATH

For this decoration you need a paper plate, scissors, red and green tissue paper, glue, red crepe paper, and a stapler.

1. Cut out the inside circle area on a paper plate.

2. Cut several small (1½″ × 1½″) squares of green tissue paper. (You'll need enough squares to cover the paper plate rim.)

3. Cut six 1″ squares of red tissue paper. Trim corners of squares so they are round.

4. Glue green squares to the paper plate rim. (Green squares should be placed close together).

5. When rim is entirely covered with green tissue paper, space and glue red circles to rim wreath.

6. Make a big red crepe paper bow. Staple bow to the bottom of the wreath.

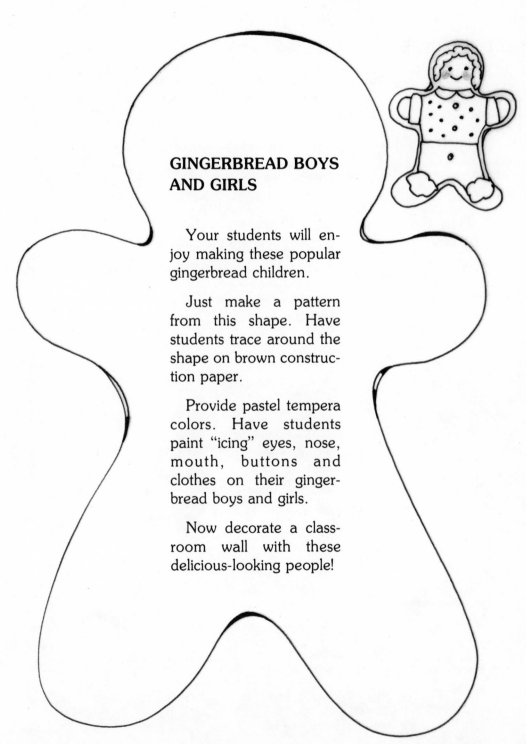

## GINGERBREAD BOYS AND GIRLS

Your students will enjoy making these popular gingerbread children.

Just make a pattern from this shape. Have students trace around the shape on brown construction paper.

Provide pastel tempera colors. Have students paint "icing" eyes, nose, mouth, buttons and clothes on their gingerbread boys and girls.

Now decorate a classroom wall with these delicious-looking people!

## DOORKNOB DECORATIONS

Your classroom door can look inviting at Christmas time! To make a doorknob decoration you'll need: construction paper, fabric scraps, yarn, scissors, glue, and glitter.

1. Cut any Christmas shape from construction paper.

2. Somewhere on the shape draw a circle a little larger than the door-knob.

3. Place the scissors inside the circle and cut out the circle area. Then cut ½″ long slits from the center circle area as illustration shows.

4. Decorate shape using colored paper, fabric scraps, glitter, etc.

5. Slip decoration over the doorknob.

## PAPER ROLL SANTA

Each student will enjoy making his own Santa Claus! You'll need: empty cardboard bathroom tissue rolls, red paper, colored paper scraps, cotton, and glue.

1. Cover the cardboard roll with red paper.

2. Use colored paper scraps to add face, cap, arms, boots, etc.

3. To make the beard, glue on cotton.

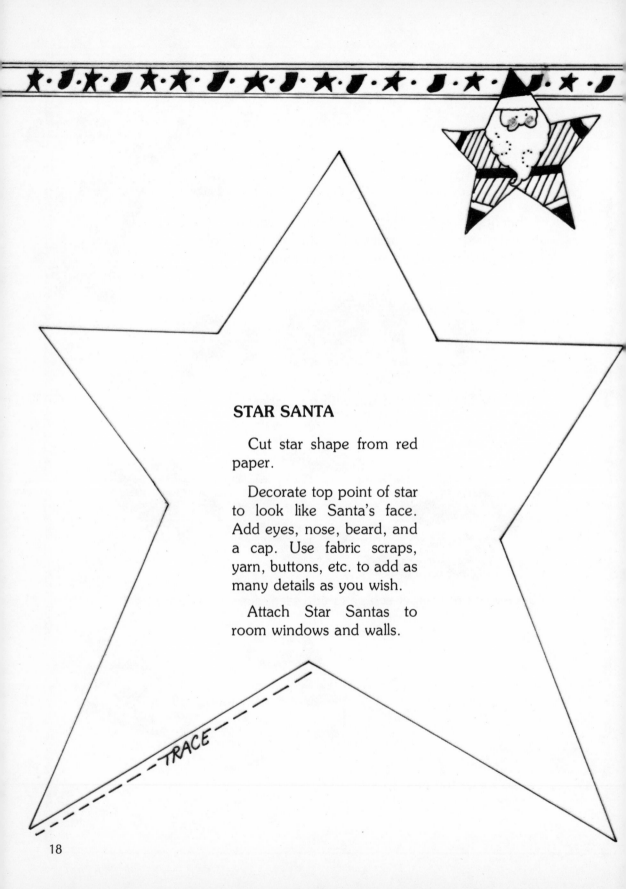

### STAR SANTA

Cut star shape from red paper.

Decorate top point of star to look like Santa's face. Add eyes, nose, beard, and a cap. Use fabric scraps, yarn, buttons, etc. to add as many details as you wish.

Attach Star Santas to room windows and walls.

TRACE

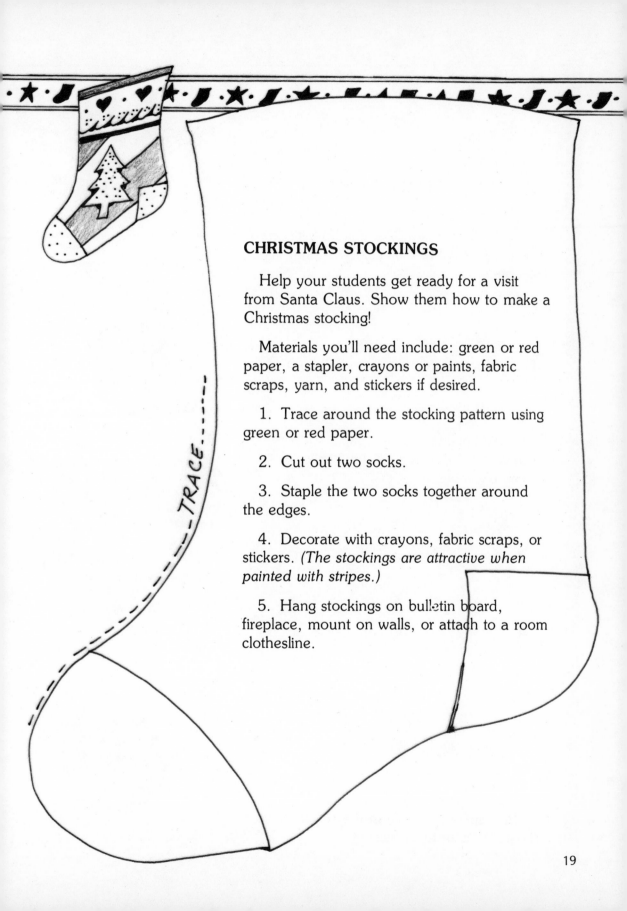

## CHRISTMAS STOCKINGS

Help your students get ready for a visit from Santa Claus. Show them how to make a Christmas stocking!

Materials you'll need include: green or red paper, a stapler, crayons or paints, fabric scraps, yarn, and stickers if desired.

1. Trace around the stocking pattern using green or red paper.

2. Cut out two socks.

3. Staple the two socks together around the edges.

4. Decorate with crayons, fabric scraps, or stickers. *(The stockings are attractive when painted with stripes.)*

5. Hang stockings on bulletin board, fireplace, mount on walls, or attach to a room clothesline.

TRACE

# CHRISTMAS SPARKLE BALL

For this decoration you need a balloon, glue, tissue paper (Christmas colors), string, glitter, and scissors.

1. Blow up balloon to size desired and tie off. (Leave about a 10″ string on balloon.)

2. Add pieces of tissue paper—wet with watered down glue—until balloon is entirely covered.

3. Sprinkle glitter over the balloon.

4. Let the balloon dry in a suspended position for one day.

5. Let air out of balloon after it is completely dry.

Hang sparkle balls from the ceiling or on a classroom Christmas tree.

## POM-POM WREATHS

For each pom-pom wreath, you will need cardboard, scissors, yarn, a styrofoam wreath form, T-pins (found at craft stores), a large bow, a cardboard tube from paper towels, Christmas wrapping paper, orange or yellow tissue paper.

Here is the procedure.

1. Cut cardboard forms to use in making the pom-poms. For each student, cut two circles, each 4 inches in diameter with a 2-inch hole in the center.

2. Put two circles together. Wrap with several layers of yarn, as shown.

3. Cut through the yarn around the circumference of the yarn circle.

4. Carefully work a thin piece of yarn in between the two cardboard circles. Bring the yarn all the way around inside the circles. Tie the two ends of the yarn together and pull tight around the cut yarn pieces. Tie a strong knot.

5. Carefully remove the cardboard forms. Fluff the yarn into a ball. Trim any long pieces, to make the pom-pom symmetrical. Make enough pom-poms to cover the wreath form.

6. Using T-pins, pin the pom-poms to the styrofoam wreath form. Add a large ribbon bow. Tie a piece of yarn around the wreath, at the top, for a hanger.

7. Cut a piece of the cardboard tube short enough to fit inside the wreath. Cover the tube with Christmas wrapping paper so it looks like a candle. Add a tissue-paper flame.

8. Cut notches in the sides of the tube, so it will slip over the stryrofoam. Fasten the tube in place with T-pins.

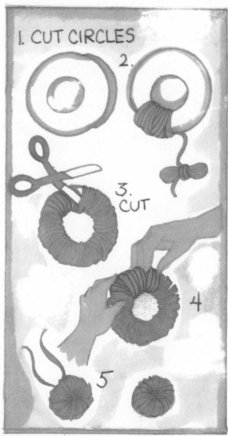

# TREE TRIMS FROM NATURE

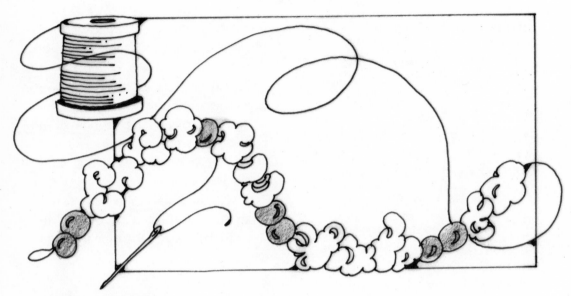

## TREE CHAINS

Obtain popcorn still on the cob. (You might find it at a farm or natural foods store.) Let students pick the kernels off the cob. Pop the corn as a class activity. Then bring in some fresh cranberries. Show students how to string the cranberries and popcorn together with a needle and thread. Then wrap your special Christmas chain around your classroom tree!

## ACORN BELLS

Collect clusters of acorns from oak trees. Carefully remove the nuts, leaving only the caps. Decorate each cluster of caps with a red or green yarn bow. Glue a dried pea in each shell as the clanger. Add a string at the top for hanging.

## WALNUT ELVES AND SANTAS

Collect old walnut shells. Glue together two walnut halves with a string looped in between them to make a hanger. Use felt or paper scraps to make a mouth, eyes, ears, etc. Cut a semi-circle of felt or paper to make a hat. Glue back edges together and then glue to top of walnut. Use cotton for hair, beards, and hat trim.

## SEED STARS

Prior to class time, provide a lightweight cardboard star for each child. Punch a hole in one point and insert a piece of yarn to use for hanging the star. Let each child cover his star with white glue and wild birdseed. You may want to make this a two-day project and cover both sides.

## A NATURAL TREE

Use pine cones, seed pods, and dried leaves collected from fall nature walks to decorate your classroom tree.

Paint the pods and leaves with bright colors. Then sprinkle them with glitter while the paint is still wet. When the decorations dry, hang each one on the tree, tying it on with a red ribbon.

## MILKWEED POD PETS

Your pupils will enjoy making a variety of milkweed pod pets. These amusing decorations are simple to make. Just paint the outside of each pod. Use paper, felt, and fabric scraps to add detail. Paint on eyes or add moveable eyes (available at most craft stores.) Use strong thread to hang the creatures from the tree.

## PINE CONE PEOPLE

Pine cone people are fun and easy to make. And they'll add a natural look to your classroom Christmas tree. Glue a small nut on top of a cone to make a head. Use colored markers to draw on features. For hair, add cotton, natural wool or yarn. Twist a pipe cleaner around cone for arms or glue on dried leaves. To hang your pine cone person, glue a loop of string to back of the cone.

# BULLETIN BOARDS

Use your bulletin boards to capture the special colors, smells, sights and sounds of Christmas!

## CHRISTMAS SIGHTS

Bring a sparkling Christmas tree into your classroom via a bulletin board. First cover the board with white paper. Cut out a large evergreen tree from construction paper and attach it to the board. Have students make paper ornaments. They may want to decorate the ornaments with glitter before attaching them to the tree. Students may also enjoy drawing colorful gifts to put under the tree. Talk about the special sights at Christmas time.

## CHRISTMAS SMELLS

Your students will enjoy making this tantalizingly good bulletin board. It's filled with Christmas things that have those special Christmassy smells! Attach things like evergreen sprigs, candy canes, a string of cranberries and popcorn, a cotton ball dabbed in vanilla, cinnamon sticks, whole cloves, etc. Use the bulletin board as a springboard for discussing special smells associated with Christmas.

## CHRISTMAS COLORS

Create a window out of a bulletin board showing the colors of Christmas this December. First cover the board with white paper. Divide the board into squares that look like panes. Have pupils cut out and decorate different objects that show the traditional Christmas colors. Mount the pictures in the panes. For a snow-like effect, tape cotton or polyester fill (used for stuffing toys) around the panes.

## CHRISTMAS SOUNDS (art on page 29)

"Merry Christmas" sounds different in the various languages spoken around the world. Let your pupils experiment with other languages. Print "Merry Christmas" on the bulletin board. Then below it print the same sentiment in other languages. Illustrate your bulletin board by showing a child dressed to represent his/her native country next to that country's "Merry Christmas." Help pupils learn to say "Merry Christmas" in several languages.

# MERRY CHRISTMAS

## CHRISTMAS ANIMALS ON PARADE

Ask students to make or bring in pictures of animals they associate with Christmas. You should get a good collection of sheep, camels, bears, chipmunks, reindeer, cows, mice, etc. Mount the pictures. Cover the bulletin board with gold paper. Make a colorful caption of red and green letters for your bulletin board: "CHRISTMAS ANIMALS ON PARADE." You may also want to cut some borders to make the bulletin board section look like circus wagons. Use Christmas colors. Display the pictures in the "wagons." Use bulky craft yarn for the bars. Then take some time to read a few animal Christmas stories and play some animal Christmas records.

# LEARNING CENTERS

## STORY STOCKING

Second graders and advanced first graders will enjoy this creative writing project. Stuff a Christmas stocking full of ideas. Have pupils choose one idea about which to write a poem or short story. Here are some ideas.

- Name an elf and describe its personality.

- Tell about a snowman who comes to life. (Tell what he does and where he goes.)

- If you could be one of Santa's reindeer, which one would you be? Why?

- If you were a Christmas present, what would you be?

- Write about Christmas colors, sounds, or smells.

## THE ALPHABET TREE

Kindergarteners will especially enjoy decorating a tree or large branch with letters of the alphabet. Cut out block letters and let pupils decorate the letters with pieces of felt, calico, wrapping paper, or burlap. Pupils may also want to add glitter and sequins to their letters for a festive look.

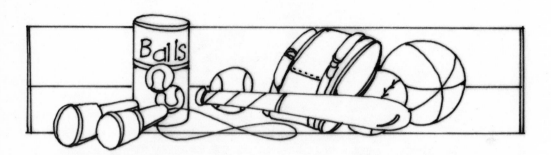

## CHRISTMAS CUSTOMERS

Let your second grade pupils test their vocabulary and association skills in an enjoyable way. Choose a pupil to be a store owner. Other students are customers. Each player will need a pencil and paper. The store owner will say something such as "I run a sport store, and I sell B; what will you buy?" Each player must make a list of everything he can think of to buy from that store which begins with the letter "b." The winner is the player with the longest list in a given amount of time. Examples of purchases from the sport store might be: balls, bat, belt, backpack, boots, boat, box kite, boomerang, binoculars, basketball, etc. Students will enjoy taking turns being a store owner.

## GIFTS FOR SANTA

All primary pupils will enjoy making pictures for Santa while you test their small muscle coordination skills. Have pupils draw, color and paint pictures for Santa. Then mail the pictures to Santa at the North Pole. Drawing ideas: reindeer, Santa in a sleigh; Mrs. Claus helping Santa put on his suit; busy elves in Santa's workshop, etc.

## THE PRICE IS RIGHT

Introduce comparative shopping to your first and second graders. Have them cut out pictures of things they like from a variety of catalogs and magazines. (Include discount store sale ads as well as expensive department store ads.) Mount the items on construction paper and attach a price to each.

Have other students make pretend money—coins and bills. Give each pupil the same amount of money and let them choose and buy items of their choice.

Let pupils take turns showing and telling what they bought with their money. Encourage pupils to tell why they chose a certain item over another and discuss the different costs involved.

## "I CAN DO IT!" POSTERS

Give each pupil a large sheet of construction paper. Suggest that students draw or cut out pictures from old magazines showing some of the things they can do—run, read, sing, do errands, talk, etc. Label each poster "Things I Can Do." Have pupils show their posters and talk about them. Encourage the students to use their abilities as Christmas gifts for their parents, brothers, sisters, grandparents, neighbors, and friends.

# GAMES AND RHYTHMIC ACTIVITIES

## THE SNOWFLAKE GAME

PROCEDURE: Students divide into groups of three except for one child who stays out of the groups. In each group of three, two students join hands to form a Christmas tree. The third child is the snowflake, and stands between them. The child not in a group is called the extra snowflake.

TO PLAY: Tell the students that the extra snowflake is looking for a Christmas tree. Each time you hear the verse: "Run, little snowflake, one, two, three. Run and find a new Christmas tree," all the snowflakes must find new trees. The student who doesn't find a tree, becomes the extra snowflake.

## TOY PARADE

PROCEDURE: Each student decides what toy he'd like to be. Students draw pictures or letter words on sheets of paper telling what toys they are. Students fasten string or yarn to their pictures so they can wear the signs.

TO PLAY: The teacher plays parade music. Students march around the room making movements and gestures to indicate what toys they are. That is, a child pretending he's a toy airplane, should stretch out his arms like wings. A child pretending to be a rag doll, should make his arms go flippity-flop.

## JINGLE-BELL DANCE

PROCEDURE: Each student chooses a partner. One child is a reindeer. One is Santa. Each reindeer puts jingle bell reins* around his waist and under his arms. Santa holds the jingle-bell reins.

TO PLAY: The teacher plays music ("Rudolph, the Red-Nosed Reindeer" or other Christmas songs) while the reindeer and Santas sing and dance around the room. Partners change places so that all students have a turn at being both a reindeer and a Santa.

*To make jingle bell reins, simply attach small bells to a strip of fabric or a heavy piece of rug yarn.

## SANTA'S HELPERS

PROCEDURE: Have your primary pupils form a large circle to play this Christmas charades game.

TO PLAY: Select one pupil to start the game. That pupil should stand in the center of the circle and pretend that he or she is one of Santa's helpers. The child acts out making a toy for Santa. The other students try to guess what toy he is making. The first student to guess correctly becomes Santa's helper, and he starts pretending to make a different toy.

## VILLAGE CHRISTMAS TREE

PROCEDURE: Mark off two parallel lines as far apart as possible—20 feet or more between. Choose one player to be the village Christmas tree. The "tree" stands with his heels to one line, his back to the other players. Other players line up behind the other line with their toes to the line.

TO PLAY: At the signal to go, the tree counts to ten as loudly as possible and then turns quickly around. While he is counting, each player moves toward the village line as quickly as possible, putting one foot in front of the other with heel to toe in each step. By the time the tree reaches the ten count, players must freeze. If the tree catches anyone moving, that person must return to the starting line and begin again. The winner is the first person to make it across the line into the village. He then becomes the tree, and the first tree joins the other players.

# THINGS
# TO MAKE
# AND DO

# GRAB AN IDEA

Here are quickie Christmas gift ideas. All can be made easily with materials that are readily available.

*1. To make floating Christmas candles.* Melt wax. Pour melted wax into small metal gelatin molds. Use Christmas shapes. Add wicks as the wax starts to set. Unmold. Float your small candles in a glass dish half-filled with water.

*2. To make hanging flower balls.* Insert dried straw flowers into a styrofoam ball, to cover it. Add a bow. Add ribbon, with which to hang the ball.

*3. To make a miniature bouquet.* Put florist's clay in the lid of a small, pretty jar. Arrange dried flowers in the clay. Then screw on the jar over the flowers. You'll have a miniature bouquet under glass.

*4. To make fancy soap.* Moisten a bar of soap. Apply a decal. Allow to dry. Coat the decal area with melted paraffin.

*5. To decorate a candle.* Wash a candle in detergent. Mix together one teaspoon of water, one teaspoon of white glue, and one drop of detergent. Sponge mixture on candle, then apply a small decal.

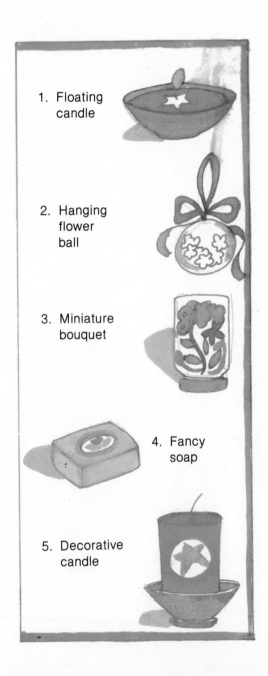

1. Floating candle

2. Hanging flower ball

3. Miniature bouquet

4. Fancy soap

5. Decorative candle

*6. Stationery.* Provide self-stick seals, ribbons, plain paper, and envelopes. Create matching cards and envelopes with simple but elegant designs—trees, stars, etc.

*7. Christmas baskets.* Paint small baskets. Fill with greens, flowers, candy.

*8. Christmas boxes.* Wrap tiny boxes to look like Christmas presents. Use the boxes to decorate a Christmas tree.

*9. Trees.* Cut trees from salt-flour dough. Put a hanger hole in each one. Let dry (3-4 days). Paint.

*10.* Santa hats. Make red felt cones. Decorate with cotton to look like Santa's hats. Add hanger. Turn over, and fill with Christmas goodies.

*11. Patchwork balls.* Provide small scraps of colorful cotton fabric, styrofoam balls, table knives, and small nails. Let a pupil push the edge of a piece of fabric into a styrofoam ball, using a knife. Continue around the edge until all of edge is inserted. Do the same with a second piece of fabric, then a third, etc., until entire ball is covered. Push loop of yarn into top, with nail, to make a hanger.

6. Stationery

7. Baskets

8. Boxes

9. Trees

10. Santa hats

11. Patchwork balls

# MAKE A CRÈCHE

Help each child make a crèche to take home and use. You can use homemade clay and let each child shape the figures as he desires. Mix together 4 cups of flour, 1 cup of salt, and 1½ cups of water. Knead until smooth. Store in an airtight container. Bake the figures at 325° for 45 minutes, then paint with poster paints.

You may prefer to purchase a kit of plaster molds. Begin pouring the plaster several weeks ahead of time. Spray figures with gold paint, or paint them in colors with tempera.

Simple crèche figures also can be made from paper. Use paper cups, construction paper, pieces of gold foil, etc. Let the students use their imaginations in making appropriate figures.

# OLD-FASHIONED ORNAMENTS

You will need several kinds of gift wrapping paper with a pattern on both sides; scissors; pencils.

Here is the procedure:

1. Make several heavy cardboard patterns of a star, a bell, and a circle. (Trace the shapes on this page.)

2. Let pupils draw around the patterns, making many stars, bells, and circles from the wrapping paper. Have them cut out the shapes.

3. For each ornament, you'll need ten pieces of the same shape and same color. Let pupils assemble the shapes in groups of ten.

4. This last step, you will have to do. Use a sewing machine, set at the longest stitch setting. Carefully adjust the tension. Sew each group of ten shapes together, down the center. Tie the thread together at the bottom and cut off. Leave long strands of thread at the top. Tie the thread together just above the shape, and again about three inches above the shape. Use this thread as hanger.

5. Open out the shapes, so they form 3-D ornaments.

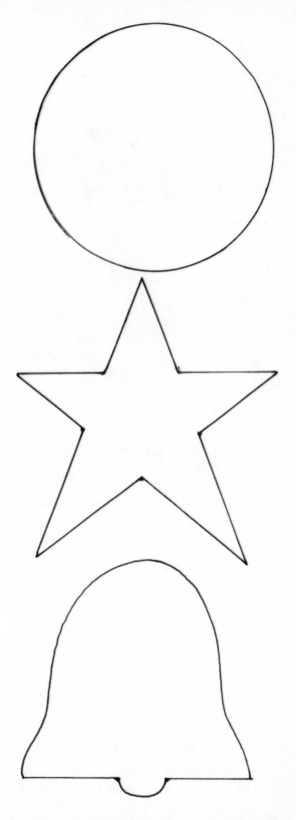

# CHRISTMAS VASE

You will need one small glass jar (such as a spice jar or salad dressing jar) for each child, and amounts of white glue, waxed paper, Q-tips, bulky yarn, and assorted small Christmas decorations and ornaments, according to the size of your group.

Here is the procedure.

1. Put a puddle of white glue on a piece of waxed paper. Using Q-tips as brushes, coat bottom of jar with glue.

2. Anchor yarn in center of bottom of jar, and wrap yarn around and around, until bottom of jar is covered. Press yarn into glue, so it will hold.

3. Cover sides of jar with glue.

4. Keep wrapping the yarn around, to cover sides of jar, from bottom to top. Press yarn into glue, so it will hold.

5. When jar is covered, cut off yarn and tuck end in. Add bows, plastic greenery, small ornaments, as available.

# DIPPING CANDLES

Step 1: melt the wax. An adult should handle this process. Put wax (paraffin) in a coffee can. It you want to tint the candles, add wax crayons or stubs of old colored candles. Put water, to about an inch, in a sauce pan wider than the coffee can. Place the coffee can in this sauce pan. Heat over low heat, until paraffin melts.

Step 2: dip the candles. Set up three or four separate work places. At each, place a coffee can of melted wax beside a can or bowl of cold water. Be sure there is a flat surface nearby. Provide candlewicking, cut in 10-inch lengths. Tie a small weight at one end of a wick. The child holds the wicking at the other end and dips it into the wax. Then he dips it into the cold water. Next, he hand rolls the wick to press in the paraffin. The child repeats this process a number of times, until the desired diameter is attained. Instruct children to dip quickly and evenly. Discard weight when finished.

Be sure children understand how hot the wax is! Guard against carelessness.

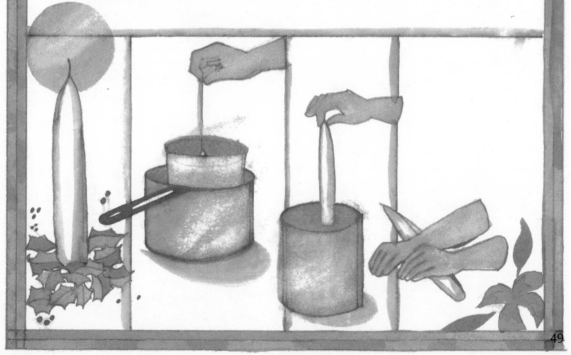

# KEEPSAKE
# ORNAMENTS

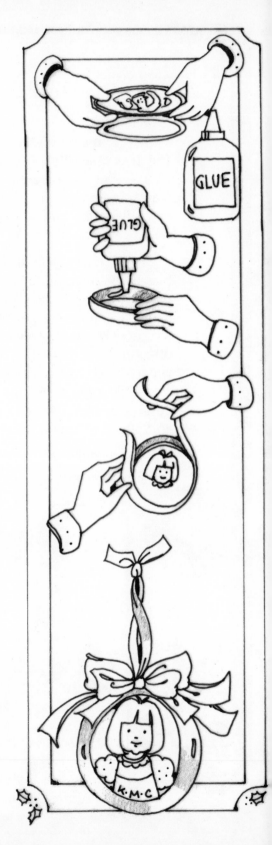

For each child you will need one two-piece canning lid, two yards of white lace seam binding. You will also need quantities of red seam binding, cardboard, glue, several pairs of scissors, and a stapler. Ask each child to bring in a wallet-sized school photo.

1. Place flat part of lid over the photo, centering photo underneath. Draw around edges, and cut off extra part of photo. (If photo is too small, glue it to red paper, and then draw the circle.)

2. Using flat part of lid as a pattern, draw and cut out a circle of cardboard.

3. Glue photo to cardboard. Glue cardboard to flat part of canning lid, on inside of lid. Let glue dry.

4. Cut a strip of red seam binding about 18 inches long. This will be the hanger for the ornament.

5. Spread glue on inside of lid rim. Thread hanger ribbon through, so lid is about in center of red binding. Insert photo, so lid forms a frame around it.

6. Cut white lace and red binding to go around lid rim. Glue red binding onto lid, around the rim. Ends should overlap at top. Then place several dots of glue on red binding. Wrap white lace around, on top of glue. Glue overlapping lace ends at top.

7. Make a floppy bow of white lace and red binding. Position it on top. Bring ends of hanger up and tie.

50

MUSIC AND DRAMA

# Share Your Love

Paulette Lutz Glenn

Paulette Lutz Glenn

1. Share your love this Christ-mas! Share it ev'-ry-where.
2. Share your love at all times! Not just on hol-i-days.

When you help and sing and give, let oth-ers see you care!
For your love, when it is shared, comes back in oth-er ways.

# I Can Be a Christmas Star

Paulette Lutz Glenn

Paulette Lutz Glenn

Do actions as follows: "I can be a Christmas star!" (Point to self.) "I've five points...." (Hold up 5 fingers.) "Fingertips" (wiggle fingers,) "my toes, my head." (point to each.) "I'm a twinkling star." (Rock forward and back.) Children might make large cardboard stars to wear as they sing the song.

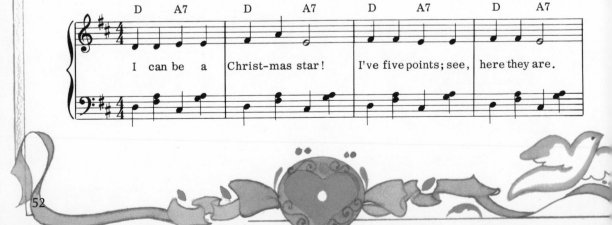

I can be a Christ-mas star! I've five points; see, here they are.

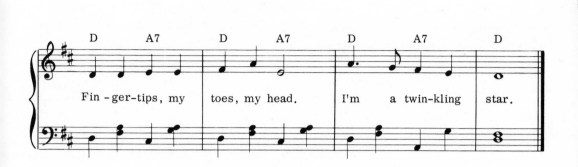

Fin - ger-tips, my  toes, my head.  I'm  a  twin-kling  star.

## Snowflakes

Paulette Lutz Glenn

Paulette Lutz Glenn

**Slowly, gently**

Lit - tle snow-flakes, big-ger snow-flakes, man - y shapes and  man-y  si - zes.

*Note:  etc.

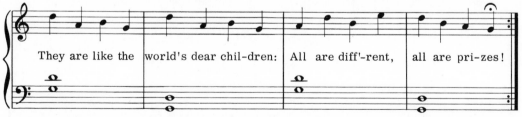

They are like the world's dear chil-dren:  All  are diff'-rent,  all are pri-zes!

Snowflakes, built on a pentatonic scale, could be played on all five black keys, by flatting every note.

*Jingle bells played on each quarter-pulse give a nice effect.

# Ding! Dong! Little Bell

Paulette Lutz Glenn                                    Paulette Lutz Glenn

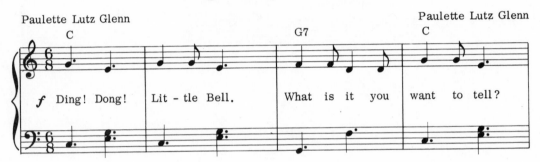

f Ding! Dong! | Lit - tle Bell. | What is it you | want to tell?

"Christ - mas, | Oh, it's fun!" | rings the lit - tle | bell.

Optional Handbell or Orff instrument accompaniment for Ding! Dong! Little Bell

or

54

# CHRISTMAS MAGIC

*by Jane Belk Moncure*

*Note to the Teacher:* This one act playlet needs few props and very little scenery. (See props list on page 62.) The play can involve an entire class or just a few boys and girls. You can have as many elves, snowflakes, fir trees, reindeer, and star fairies as your class size allows.

Costumes can be simple. Santa might wear a bright red sweater. Mrs. Claus might wear a red apron. The elves can make and wear bright green paper hats. The snowflakes can tape little paper snowflakes on their fingers and clothes. The fir trees can tape strips of green paper branches on their arms. The reindeer characters might wear brown construction paper horns attached to a head band. Each star fairy might wear a large paper star hat or carry a star-shaped wand. The characters portraying children in the play should wear regular school clothes.

*Cast of Characters:*

| | | | |
|---|---|---|---|
| Narrator | Fir Trees | Star Fairies | Elves |
| Santa Claus | Reindeer | Children | Snowflakes |
| Mrs. Claus | | | |

TIME: The week before Christmas.

SETTING: Santa's workshop.
(There are worktables and several workbenches in the room. Some toys are on the tables. Paper hammers, saws, and pieces of wood are on the tables.)

All the elves have fallen asleep. Some are sleeping on the floor. Some have their heads resting on the tables.

The narrator is seated downstage on the right, and reads from a large book.

NARRATOR: One cold winter, Santa had a problem. All of his elves had fallen asleep. They had slept through October, and November and on into December! Santa did not know what to do! Who would help make all the toys for girls and boys? Santa tried and tried to wake up his sleeping elves, but they would not open their eyes! Now it was Christmas week! Something had to be done at once!

SANTA *(enters on the run, holding an alarm clock)*: Wake up! Wake up! Do you know what time it is? It is nearly Christmas Eve.

*(Santa shakes a few sleeping elves.).*

MRS. CLAUS *(enters shaking her head):* The alarm clock will not wake them up! You have been ringing it for weeks! It will take special Christmas magic to wake up your sleeping elves!

SANTA *(puts alarm clock on the worktable):* Christmas magic! That's it. Yes, there is a magic word for Christmas. Great Grandfather Claus told me, long ago. But I have forgotten the magic word. Oh dear!

MRS. CLAUS: Maybe the snowflakes can help you. Maybe the snowflakes know the magic word for Christmas.

SANTA *(runs to the left):* I will call my snowflakes.

> Jingle jangle
> jumble jum,
> come snowflakes,
> come!

SNOWFLAKES *(enter left stage dancing as they drop paper snowflakes around the sleeping elves. They gather around Santa and Mrs. Claus):*

SANTA: My elves are all asleep. I cannot wake them up. Who will make the Christmas toys for girls and boys? Do you know the magic word for Christmas? It will take the magic word to wake them up.

SNOWFLAKES *(all together, holding up the word SNOW and sprinkling more snowflakes):* Is the magic word for Christmas, SNOW?

*(Elves do not awaken.)*

SANTA *(looking at elves):* No!

FIRST SNOWFLAKE *(holding up the word SNOWMAN)*: Could it be SNOWMAN?

*(Elves do not move.)*

SANTA: No!

SECOND SNOWFLAKE *(holding up word SNOWBALL)*: How about SNOWBALL?

*(Elves remain quiet.)*

SANTA: Those are nice Christmas words, but not one is the magic word!

*(Snowflakes dance to far right of stage and sit down.)*

MRS. CLAUS: Maybe the fir trees can help you. Maybe they know the magic word for Christmas.

SANTA *(runs to the left)*: I will call my fir trees.

Jingle jangle
jumble jum,
come fir trees,
come!

FIR TREES *(enter left stage with paper Christmas tree decorations and gather around Santa and Mrs. Claus.)*

SANTA: As you can see, my elves are all asleep. This is a terrible problem because I need their help! I must find the magic word for Christmas to wake them up! Do you know the magic word?

FIR TREES *(holding up words CHRISTMAS TREE)*: The magic words must be . . . CHRISTMAS TREE!

*(Elves do not move.)*

SANTA: No! That's not it!

FIRST FIR TREE *(holds up words)*: How about CANDY CANES?

SECOND FIR TREE *(holds up word)*: How about TOYS?

*(Elves do not move.)*

SANTA: Those are nice Christmas words, but not one is the magic word for Christmas!

*(Fir trees go to right side of stage.)*

MRS. CLAUS: I know! Perhaps your own reindeer can help you!

SANTA *(jumps up and runs to left stage)*:

Jingle jangle
jumble jum,
come my reindeer,
come!

*(Reindeer gallop in and cluster around Santa.)*

SANTA: You are my faithful reindeer. Maybe you know the magic word for Christmas. We *must* have the magic word to wake up the elves!

REINDEER *(all together, holding up the word and ringing little bells)*: The magic word must be BELLS!

*(Elves do not move.)*

FIRST REINDEER *(holding up word)*: How about the word SLEIGH?

*(Elves stay still.)*

SANTA: Those are nice Christmas words, but not one is the magic word!

*(Reindeer gallop to left side of stage.)*

58

SANTA: Oh! What shall I do? What shall I do?

MRS. CLAUS: Why don't you ask the children, Santa? Surely the children know the magic word for Christmas.

SANTA: But the children are far away, and it is nighttime.

MRS. CLAUS: The star fairies can find them.

SANTA: Of course! The star fairies! They will find the children.

Jingle jangle
jumble jum,
come star fairies,
come!

*(Star fairies enter from either side depending on how many children in this group.)*

SANTA: As you can see, my elves are all asleep. They will wake up when I find the magic word for Christmas. We think the children know the magic word. You must go and find the children! Bring them to me! Hurry! Hurry!

*(The star fairies walk off stage into the audience. The star fairies lead children—previously chosen and who have rehearsed the song—to Santa.)*

SANTA: My elves are all asleep. There will be no Christmas toys this year for girls and boys *unless* you know the magic word for Christmas! Do you?

CHILDREN *(all together)*: We *think* we know the magic word.

SANTA: Tell us! Tell us the magic word!

CHILDREN *(Facing audience hold up the word LOVE as they sing the song)*:

"The magic word for Christmas is L-O-V-E, LOVE.

The magic word for Christmas is L-O-V-E, LOVE.

Christmas trees are very nice,
So are reindeer, snow, and ice,
but the magic word for Christmas
   is L-O-V-E, LOVE!"

# The Magic Word for Christmas

Jane Belk Moncure

Jane Belk Moncure

The mag - ic word for Christ -
mas is L - O - V - E, Love.
The mag - ic word for Christ -

*(As the children sing, the elves wake up, dance around and begin making toys at the worktable.)*

SANTA: Love! That's the magic word for Christmas! Let's sing it again!

*(Everyone on stage sings the little song.)*

SANTA: Oh! But I will need more help this year! My Christmas elves cannot possibly make all the toys for girls and boys!

SNOWFLAKES *(all together)*: We will help you!

FIR TREES *(all together)*: We will help you!

REINDEER *(all together)*: We will help you, Santa!

STAR FAIRIES *(all together)*: You can count on us!

SANTA *(facing audience with children around him)*: And . . . you out there . . . will you help me by spreading the magic word for Christmas? What is it?

(Hopefully the audience re-sponds with the word "love.")

SANTA: Great! Let's all sing the magic song!

*(The cast sings "The Magic Word for Christmas" as they walk into the audience and pass out little cards they have made that carry the word, "LOVE.")*

*The End.*

## PROPS

*Santa:* an alarm clock

*Narrator:* large book

*Snowflakes:* colorful posters with words: SNOW, SNOWMAN, SNOWBALL

*Fir trees:* colorful posters with the words: CHRISTMAS TREE, CANDY CANES, TOYS; paper Christmas tree decorations

*Reindeer:* colorful posters with the words: BELLS, SLEIGH; little bells

*Children:* colorful posters with the word: "LOVE"

Every member of the cast can make small, colorful cards that carry the word "LOVE". The cards will be passed out to the audience at the end of the play. These cards can be kept in the actors' pockets until the end of the play.

CUSTOMS
AND
TRADITIONS

Why not let your pupils learn about some of the Christmas customs and traditions by making a giant mural? Using butcher paper and paints, let pupils illustrate some of the customs and traditions discussed in this section.

## THE CHRISTMAS TREE

One of the oldest and most popular traditions involves the Christmas tree. And there are a lot of different stories about the famous tree. Some say the custom of decorating an evergreen tree comes from ancient Rome. The Romans used to decorate trees during their winter Saturnalia celebration—a festival honoring their mythical gods of the sun and land.

Others say that Martin Luther, a German minister, had the first Christmas tree. The story goes that one starry Christmas Eve, Luther walked among the evergreens. As he walked, he felt he could see the stars shining on the trees. He wanted to share the joy he felt with his family. So he cut down and took home a small fir tree. He decorated it with small candles to represent the stars. Luther said the glowing tree stood for Christ who is the Light of the world.

And still others say that once, long ago, a poor forester took care of a lonely child. The Christ child appeared and touched a fir tree beside the forester's cottage. The tree sparkled with tiny lights and became the first Christmas tree.

Today, many people decorate artificial trees rather than live trees. But whether live or not, putting up a Christmas tree is a tradition that has spread and is enjoyed the world over.

## SUGGESTED ACTIVITIES

1. *Decorate a small tree.* Let pupils take it to a shut-in (perhaps a sick class member).

2. *Put on a play.* Guide the children in presenting a play about the story of Martin Luther's first Christmas tree.

3. *Decorate a tree in your classroom.* You may want to let the children make the ornaments.

## EVERGREENS

Evergreens have long been a symbol of everlasting life—even before the Christian era. The ancient people of Celtic and Nordic lands almost worshipped the greens "that do not die" — greens which give promise that spring will come again. The early Romans, for the celebration of their winter feast, the Saturnalia, generously decorated their homes with green boughs, garlands and flowers.

Pine, spruce, fir, holly, mistletoe, ivy, and juniper are some of the greens that are used for Christmas decorations today. Mistletoe especially adds to the fun at

Christmas time. In many countries, mistletoe is hung above doorways. And anyone caught walking under the mistletoe must give a kiss to the person catching him.

## SUGGESTED ACTIVITY

1. *Decorate the classroom.* Use evergreen branches and holly.

## LIGHTS

Decorating with lights is another way we add to our Christmas joy. And candles were a part of the ancient Saturnalia tradition. Martin Luther (the German minister) first used candles on Christmas trees to represent the stars above Bethlehem on the night of Christ's birth. Ireland is one of many countries where the people put candles in their windows. According to Irish lore, the Irish put lighted candles in their windows on Christmas Eve to welcome all who, like Mary and Joseph of old, may be in search of shelter. Legend says that only those with the name "Mary" may blow out the candles.

## SUGGESTED ACTIVITIES

1. *Plan a candlelight party* for your children. Or choose a favorite poem or short story to read to them by candlelight.

2. *Make candles.* See page 49 for instructions.

## THE YULE LOG

The Yule log is associated closely with English traditions. It is usually a piece of a sturdy oak tree. The Yule log is burned at Christmas. Then, for good luck, part of it is saved and used to light the log for the following Christmas.

## CHRISTMAS CAROLS

Christmas carols also came about long ago. Some say they began with the singing of the angels, as told in the Bible story. Whether heavenly or human, singing has always been a way of showing joy.

"Silent Night," one of the most famous of all Christmas carols, was written in the little town of Oberndorn, Austria. That was way back in 1818. It was nearing Christmas and the town's church organ was broken. Everyone was worried that there might not be any Christmas music. A man named Joseph Mohr walked through quiet fields one night, thinking about the broken organ. As he walked, the words for the song "Silent Night" came to

him. Another man, Franz Gruber, wrote the music. Gruber played it on his guitar that Christmas morning while Joseph Mohr sang the words.

People have been singing for years and years, but the tradition of caroling began in old England. Groups of musicians and singers went from house to house, singing songs. Today this custom is still observed in England and also in various other parts of the world. Carolers bring the holiday spirit to shoppers, shut-ins, and hospital patients.

## SUGGESTED ACTIVITY

*Take your class caroling in the school neighborhood.*

## THE CRÈCHE

Long ago, church leaders decided not only to tell but show the people about the birth of the Christ child. They created the Christmas crib, sometimes called a crèche or nativity scene. The custom of making cribs spread throughout the world. Some families today make their own nativity scenes. Figures may be made of wood, wax, plaster, paper or pottery. And sometimes churches use real people and animals to recreate the nativity scene.

## SUGGESTED ACTIVITIES

1. *Crèche Display.* Set up a creche display in your classroom.
2. *Make a Crèche.* See the instructions on page 46.

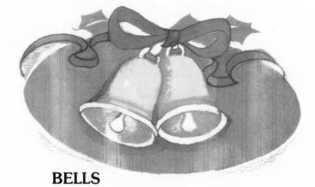

## BELLS

The joyous ringing of bells has been heard for centuries at Christmas time. The bells ring out to proclaim and celebrate the birth of the Christ child.

## SUGGESTED ACTIVITIES

1. *Make bells to decorate your classroom.*

2. *Bring in some bells.* Use them for sound effects when reading "The Night Before Christmas" or other Christmas stories. Use the bells for appropriate songs during song time.

## STOCKINGS

Hanging up stockings on Christmas Eve is a fun custom we all enjoy. But how many of you know how the custom got started? Long ago, when a fireplace was a home's only source of heat, stockings and other clothing were hung by the fire to dry. Shoes, too, were placed by the fireplace. It is said that when St. Nicholas would come down a chimney, the first thing he'd bump into were the hanging socks. So that's where he'd put his gifts for good boys and girls.

SUGGESTED ACTIVITY

1. *Make Christmas Stockings.* See the instructions on page 19.

## GIFTS

The giving of gifts has been a part of all celebrations, whether pagan, Christian or Jewish. Gift-giving is a way of demonstrating love for others. But this custom at Christmas may have come from the story of the Wise-men who brought gifts—gold, frankincense and myrrh—to baby Jesus.

### SUGGESTED ACTIVITY

1. *See the craft section,* pages 44 to 50, for gift ideas to make and give at Christmas time.

## CHRISTMAS CARDS

People of all countries enjoy sending greetings via special cards for Christmas. The first known Christmas card appeared in 1843 when an English artist designed one for the special season. The very next year, 1844, other cards were produced. Since then, all shapes and sizes of Christmas cards have been spreading joy and good wishes to all parts of the world.

### SUGGESTED ACTIVITY

*Let pupils design and make their own Christmas cards for family members and friends.*

## CHRISTMAS FOODS

Good things to eat are a part of Christmas. We celebrate this time of joy by enjoying foods and sharing them.

*(You may want to have several parents or other adults "show and tell," by bringing in special breads, cakes, or cookies that are part of their heritage, and giving each child a taste.)*

Christmas doughs and breads have had an important place in Christmas feasts in every country, because long ago when there was not much food, bread was truly important to life.

Each country has its own special Christmas foods. In old England, a boar's head, roast beef, mince pies, and plum pudding were popular. Remember Jack Horner's Christmas pie? It was a mince pie. Mince pies used to be made of chopped meats and fruit. Later, apples, raisins, molasses, suet, and spices were used. At first the pies were oblong instead of round and had a lattice crust. They were made this way to represent the manger. The apples represented hope for good crops; and the spices, the gifts of the Wise-men.

In France today, a cake is baked in the shape of a Yule log. Special Christmas cookies are baked of whole wheat flour, brown sugar, and dates. Some think it is bad luck if the Christmas cake is not first shared with a needy person.

In Holland, cakes are often baked in the shapes of animals and birds.

In Germany, kitchens are filled with the smell of Christmas cookies baking in the oven. Almost every community has its own favorite kind of cookie—gingerbread men, hard spicy cookies, honey cookies.

In Italy, a tall mound of bread flavored with citron and raisins is baked at Christmas time. Magi Cakes are eaten on Christmas Day and Magi Day.

In Norway, Sweden, and Denmark, the main dish for Christmas dinner is fish. A rich rice pudding is the usual dessert. In Norway, an almond is placed in the dish of rice pudding and the person who finds it, they say, will be the first to be married.

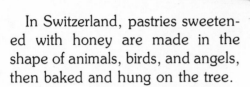

In Switzerland, pastries sweetened with honey are made in the shape of animals, birds, and angels, then baked and hung on the tree.

In the early days of America, turkey, cranberries, corn, turnips, potatoes, pumpkin pie, and fruitcake made the Christmas feast. The Christmas foods we eat today include these foods as well as foods that were brought to America by immigrants from other countries.

## SUGGESTED ACTIVITIES

1. *Bake.* Spend the last ½ hour or so of the day making cookies or bread from a recipe of another country. Have pupils participate in mixing and kneading, etc. Bake the mixture at home.

2. *Put cookies or bread* in boxes and take them to a nursing home.

# MAKE SOME DANISH COOKIES

½ cup shortening
¾ cup brown sugar (packed)
1 egg
½ cup molasses
3 drops anise oil
1 tablespoon hot water

3½ cups flour
½ teaspoon soda
½ teaspoon cinnamon
½ teaspoon cloves
¼ teaspoon salt
1/8 teaspoon pepper

Heat oven to 350°. Mix shortening, sugar, egg, molasses, anise oil, and water. Blend in remaining ingredients. Knead dough until right consistency for shaping balls.

Shape dough (about one level teaspoonful at a time) into balls. Place an inch apart on ungreased baking sheet. Bake 12 minutes or until golden brown on bottom. Makes about eight dozen cookies.

Store cookies in an airtight container. (For softer cookies, store with a slice of apple.)

# CHRISTMAS AROUND THE WORLD

*This section provides information on how Christmas is celebrated in many lands. You may want to read the story to your pupils and then have the children paint a panorama showing how Christmas is celebrated in the various countries. Pupils may also enjoy acting out the story as you read it to them. Or, choose one or more countries and let the pupils construct celebration scenes based on the specific Christmas customs and traditions of the country. (The scenes can be made on a base of heavy cardboard. Clay works well for modeling people. Use chenille wire, fabric scraps, yarn, construction paper and other craft supplies to illustrate each scene.) It may work well to divide children into groups of two or three if you choose to construct more than one scene.*

## FLIGHT CHRISTMAS

Calling all passengers. Calling all passengers. Flight CHRISTMAS is now boarding. Tickets are still available for Christmas around the world! Get your flight tickets now. See how children in other lands celebrate Christmas!

"Let's join the flight, class," says teacher, Mrs. Kane. "Single file. Up, up, up, the stairs. Choose a seat by the window. And fasten your seat belts."

"Welcome to flight CHRISTMAS," calls the pilot.

"Glad to have all of you with us today. We'll be stopping in many countries for this special Christmas flight around the world. Now sit back and relax. Our first stop will be in sunny Mexico."

*"Feliz Navidad,"* shout our Mexican friends. Children and their parents are busy decorating their

homes with bright flowers. Everyone is preparing for the special days called the Posadas.

"The Posada celebration is held to remember the birth of the Christ child," explains Juan, our new Mexican friend. "On Christmas Eve, the last night of the Posadas, we have a big party. There's always lots of things to eat and fun games to play. The piñata game is the best."

"What's the piñata game?" Sally asks Juan.

"It's a game we play with a stick and a piñata. A piñata is a clay jug full of candy and toys. The jug is covered with pretty paper. Sometimes it's in the shape of a bird or animal. To play the game, the piñata is fastened to a rope and lifted above our heads. We take turns whacking at the piñata with a long stick. When the piñata breaks, we all run to pick up the candy and toys."

"Oops," says the teacher, glancing at her watch. "It's time for us to be back on the plane. We have a long way to go."

"We're now crossing the Atlantic Ocean," calls the pilot. "Wave to the children in Spain. They're awaiting the arrival of kings who, as legend has it, travel over the land with gifts for good children. They'll receive their gifts on January 6th."

"Prepare for landing," says the flight attendant. "And get ready to wish our French friends *"Joyeaux Noel!"*

The plane sputters and lowers.

In France we meet Peter. Peter

and his friends look forward to a visit from *Le Pere Noel* (St. Nicholas in French).

*"Le Pere Noel* brings us candy, nuts, fruit and gifts," says Peter.

"Does *Le Pere Noel* come in a sleigh pulled by reindeer?" Sally asks.

"No," says Peter. "He travels on a donkey all by himself."

"Look, what's that in the sky floating down? I've got it," says Jim. "It looks like a letter . . . a letter to Father Christmas!"

"It's probably from someone in England," said Sally. "Children in England write letters to Father Christmas instead of Santa Claus. They put them in the fireplace and the burned letter pieces float up the chimney."

"I wonder what Father Christmas looks like," said Jim.

"Legend says that he is tall and thin with a long white beard. And he wears a long red robe with a fur trimmed hood," says Mrs. Kane.

"Now follow me. We have to continue our trip."

"Wow. Look at those big white mountains," says Kenny.

"They're called alps in Switzerland," says Mrs. Kane. "Father Christmas *and* his wife, Lucy, visit the boys and girls at Christmas in Switzerland," she continues.

"That's right," says the pilot. "Now watch the streets for a glimpse of Father Christmas and Lucy. The Swiss Father Christmas has a red beard and wears a long robe. Lucy has her hair in two long braids. She wears a bright silk apron over a dress of lace. She carries a bag of toys for the girls while Father Christmas has a sack full of toys for the boys."

"Prepare again for landing," calls the pilot. "We'll soon be in Germany."

*"Froëliche Weinhachten"* — "Merry Christmas" in German, shout our German friends.

"Come. Let's visit a German family. They're busy preparing for Christmas . . . and they're expecting us," says Mrs. Kane.

"Look . . . there's Fran at the door. She's waiting for us."

"Please tell us what Christmas is like in Germany," asks Sue, once the group is inside Fran's home.

"Well, see this door?" says Fran. "It's locked. No one can peek inside the room until late afternoon on Christmas Eve. That's when the door is opened. Can you guess what's inside? A beautiful spruce

tree lighted with candles and decorated with all kinds of cookie figures, animals, stars, angels, ornaments and tinsel."

"Who brings the presents to German children?" asks Jason.

"In some areas of Germany, children receive gifts from *Christkind*. In other areas *Kris Kringle* may visit. In still other places *Knecht Ruprecht* may visit," Fran's mother says.

"And in Bavaria, Germany, during the 1800's, the Lutherans had their own religious view about St. Nicholas. They believed he was a messenger who took requests from children up to heaven. Then he'd descend to earth using an umbrella. He'd bring gifts from the angels to the children," Fran's dad added.

"Before you leave Germany, you must taste some of our special Christmas ginger cookies and almond candies," says Fran, holding a plate of treats.

*"Froëliche Weinhachten"* — "Merry Christmas."

"Next stop is Holland . . . then Sweden," calls our pilot as we climb back aboard the plane.

The plane lifts into the sky. The children settle back in their seats. Some fall asleep. The pilot's voice interrupts the napping children.

"Before we land in Holland, I want to tell you a little about how the Dutch people celebrate," calls the pilot.

"Why don't you ask Hans to help you? He was born in Holland," said Mrs. Kane.

"Good idea. Okay, Hans, who comes bringing gifts and candy to the Dutch children?"

"Saint Nicholas comes on December 5 in a boat filled with gifts.

Then he rides through the streets on a white horse leaving gifts for everyone."

"And where does St. Nicholas put the candy and gifts, Hans?" asks Mrs. Kane.

"He puts the gifts inside the wooden shoes placed by the fireplace."

"Prepare for a bumpy landing," calls the pilot over the loud speaker. "Be sure your seat belts are fastened."

The plane lands. The children hurry out behind Hans.

"Follow me down Main Street," says Hans. "I'll take you to the cobbler's shop . . . and to the wood carver's toy shop."

The children enjoy a fun time of sightseeing in Holland, before they again board the plane for Sweden.

In Sweden, the children learn all about St. Lucia's Day on December 13. That is the day a young girl, selected to portray Lucia, dresses in a long white gown. She wears a crown of candles on her head and walks through the streets, giving sweet rolls to the townspeople.

"Does St. Lucia bring gifts to everyone?" asks Sally.

"No. It's *Julia Tome,* a little gnome, who brings gifts to Swedish children on Christmas Eve," the Swedish tourist guide says. "And our neighbors in Finland receive their gifts from *Joukupukki,* the Yule Goat. Finnish children like to wear long-nosed masks with curled horns and pretend they are the Yule Goat. But I'll tell you no more . . . you have a long way to go before the day is up. *God Jul!* — Merry Christmas," calls our Swedish guide.

As the plane once again lifts into the air, the children look down from the clouds and wave to their new friends below. They fly over Russia and the pilot tells the legend of Babouscka, a poor, wrinkled old woman who goes looking for the Christ Child at Christmas time in Russia.

"What country are we going to visit next?" asks Kim.

"We're going to your parents' homeland—Taiwan," said Mrs. Kane. "Sit tight. We'll be there soon."

"My grandmother told me that on Christmas Eve in Taiwan, the people dress in their most colorful costumes, carry their best lanterns, and parade up and down the streets singing Christmas carols. Then right before midnight, the skies look like our Fourth of July! Firecrackers light the sky!" said Kim.

The pupils saw many trees decorated with bright paper flowers, paper chains, and cotton snowflakes while in Taiwan.

"Now it's time to visit the islands of the Philippines," said Mrs. Kane. "It is the last stop before flying back to the States."

"Do they decorate trees in the Philippines?" asked Beth.

"Yes, they decorate trees . . . banana trees!" said a flight attendant.

Once the plane lands and the children climb out, they see several banana trees decorated for Christmas. Many homes in the Philippines are decorated, too.

Some have bright flowers. Some have flags. Some have palm branches.

On the flight back to the United States, the children fly over the Pacific Ocean and make a quick stop in Hawaii. There they are greeted by Hawaiian children dressed in grass skirts and flower necklaces called *leis*. The pupils join a Hawaiian Christmas party before reboarding Flight CHRISTMAS.

"MELE KALIKIMAKA!" — Merry Christmas!" shout the children as they wave goodbye.

Once again the plane lifts into the sky.

The children are tired but excited. They're excited about all that they've seen and heard. And they're excited and eager to get back home. They want to get ready for the Santa Claus they know and love.

As you know, he's chubby and jolly and comes down the chimney the night before Christmas. Listen for the jingle of his sleigh and his jolly "Ho, ho, ho." Maybe this Christmas Eve, you'll get a glimpse of him — red suit and all!

# TOLD
# AROUND
# THE TREE

# IN THE GREAT WALLED COUNTRY

*by Raymond MacDonald Alden*

Away at the northern end of the world, where most people suppose that there is nothing but ice and snow, is a land full of children. It is called the Great Walled Country, because all around the country is a great wall of ice, hundreds of feet thick and thousands of feet high.

Nobody who lives there ever grows up. The king and queen, the princes and the courtiers, play a great deal of the time with dolls and tin soldiers. Every night at seven o'clock they have a bowl of bread and milk and go to bed. But they make excellent rulers, and the other children are well pleased with the government.

In the Great Walled Country, they never have to buy their Christmas presents. Every year, on the day before Christmas, Grandfather Christmas (I suppose we would call him Santa Claus) goes into a great forest of Christmas trees that grows just back of the palace of the king. There he fills the trees with candy and books and toys and all sorts of good things. When night comes, all the children wrap up snugly, and go to the forest to gather gifts for their friends. Each one goes by himself so that none of his friends can see what he has gathered. And no one ever thinks of such a thing as taking a present for himself.

So Christmas time is a great holiday in that land. They have been celebrating it in this way for hundreds of years.

But there was once a time, many years ago, when the children in the Great Walled Country had a very strange Christmas. There came a visitor to the land. He was an old man, and was the first stranger for many years who had succeeded in getting over the wall.

The stranger looked so wise that the king invited him to the palace.

When this old man was told how they held their Christmas celebration, he listened gravely. Then looking wiser than ever, he said to the king:

"That is all very well, but I should think there would be an easier way. Why does not everyone get his own presents? That would save the trouble of dividing them again, and everyone would be better satisfied. He could pick out just what he wanted for himself."

This seemed to the king a very wise saying. He called all his courtiers and counselors about him, and they all agreed they had been very foolish. "We will make a proclamation," they said, "and always after this follow the new plan."

So the proclamation was made. The plan seemed as wise to the children of the country as it had to the king and the counselors. Everyone had at some time been a little disappointed with his Christmas gifts; now there would be no danger of that.

On Christmas Eve, they always had a meeting at the palace, and sang carols until ten o'clock, the time for going to the forest. On this particular night, it seemed to the king that the music was not quite so merry as usual, and that the children's eyes did not shine as gladly as in other years. But there could be no good reason for this, since everyone was expecting a better time than usual. So he thought no more of it.

There was only one person at the palace that night who was not pleased with the new proclamation about the Christmas gifts. This was a little boy named Inge, who lived with his sister. Now his sister was crippled, and had to sit all day looking out of the window from her chair. Inge had always gone to the forest on Christmas Eve and returned with his arms and pockets loaded with pretty things for his sister, which would keep her amused all the coming year.

Now, said Inge to himself, what will my sister do? The poor crippled child could not go a step toward the forest. After thinking about it a long time, Inge silently made up his mind not to obey the proclamation. He decided that it would not be wrong if, instead of taking gifts for himself, he took them altogether for his sister.

And now the chimes had struck ten. The children were making their way toward the forest in starlight so bright that it almost showed their shadows on the sparkling snow. As soon as they came to the edge of the forest, they separated, each one going by himself in the old way. Though now there was really no reason why they should have secrets from one another.

Ten minutes later, if you had been in the forest, you might have seen the children standing in dismay. For, as they looked eagerly about them, they saw no presents hanging from the branches of the evergreen trees. High and low they searched, wandering farther into the forest than ever before. But still no presents appeared.

As the children were trooping out of the forest, after hours of weary searching, some of them came upon little Inge. Over his shoulder he was carrying a bag that seemed to be full to overflowing.

"Are they not beautiful things?" he cried. "I think Grandfather Christmas was never so good to us before."

Then the children begged him to tell in what part of the forest he had found his presents. He turned back and pointed to the place where he had been. "I left many more behind than I brought away," he said. "There they are! I can see some of the things shining on the trees even from here."

"Why, what do you mean?" cried the children. "There are no presents in the forest."

"No presents!" said Inge. "I have my bag full of them." But he did not offer to show them, because he did not want the children to see that they were all for his little sister.

But when the children followed his footprints in the snow, they still saw nothing on the trees. They thought that Inge must be dreaming.

On Christmas Day there was sadness all through The Great Walled Country. But those who came to the house of Inge and his sister saw plenty of books and dolls and

beautiful toys piled up about the little crippled girl's chair. When they asked where these things came from, they were told, "Why, from the Christmas-tree forest." And they shook their heads, not knowing what it could mean.

The king held a council in the palace. He appointed a committee to visit Grandfather Christmas and see what was the matter.

The committee set out upon their journey. They had very hard work to climb the great wall of ice that lay between their country and where Grandfather Christmas lived. But at last they found themselves in the very place where Grandfather Christmas lay sound asleep.

It was hard to waken him, for he always slept one hundred days after his Christmas work was over. It was only by turning the hands of the clock around two hundred times that the committee could do anything. But at last Grandfather Christmas sat up in bed, rubbing his eyes.

"Oh, sir!" cried the prince who was in charge of the committee. "We have come from the king of the Great Walled Country, to ask why you forgot us this Christmas and left no presents in the forest."

"No presents!" said Grandfather Christmas. "I never forget anything. The presents were there. You did not see them, that's all."

But the children told him that they had searched long and carefully.

"Indeed!" said Grandfather Christmas. "And did little Inge, the boy with the crippled sister, find none?"

Then the committee were silent. They had heard of the gifts at Inge's house, and did not know what to say.

"You had better go home," said Grandfather Christmas, "and let me finish my nap. The presents were there, but they were never intended for children who were looking only for themselves. I am not surprised that you could not see them. Remember that not everything wise travelers tell you is wise." And he turned over and went to sleep again.

The committee returned silently to the Great Walled Country and told the king what they had heard. The next December, the king made another proclamation, bidding everyone to seek gifts for others, in the old way, in the Christmas-tree forest.

So that is what they have been doing ever since.

# THE CHRISTMAS ROSE

*AN OLD LEGEND*
*by Lizzie Deas*

When the Magi laid their rich offerings of myrrh, frankincense, and gold by the bed of the sleeping Christ Child, legend says that a shepherd maiden stood outside the door quietly weeping.

She, too, had sought the Christ Child. She, too, desired to bring Him gifts. But she had nothing to offer, for she was very poor indeed. In vain she had searched the countryside over for one little flower to bring Him. But she could find neither bloom nor leaf, for the winter had been cold.

And as she stood there weeping, an angel passing saw her sorrow, and stooping, he brushed aside the snow at her feet. And there sprang up on the spot a cluster of beautiful winter roses—waxen white with pink-tipped petals.

"Not myrrh, nor frankincense, nor gold," said the angel, "is offering more meet for the Christ Child than these pure Christmas roses."

Joyfully the shepherd maiden gathered the flowers and made her offering to the Holy Child.

# THE JOY OF GIVING

Somehow, not only for Christmas
   But all the long year through,
The joy that you give to others
   Is the joy that comes back to you;
And the more you spend in blessing

The poor and lonely and sad,
The more of your heart's possessing
Returns to make you glad.
    *—John Greenleaf Whittier*

# THE REAL THING

Is Christmas in Alaska
Holly-smelling, tinsel-bright?
Do bundled children bellow carols
To snowed-in towns of blinking
   light?

In Portugal do people
Wrap ribboned boxes, hang
   mistletoe,

Stir sticky fudge, string popcorn
   chains,

Forget their lines in Christmas
   shows?

I've always wondered whether
Hawaiian Christmas is like
   Christmas here.
I've heard it's more like Florida's
Where kids sunburn all year!

At home in snowy Nebraska
We trim the tree—it's a Yuletide
   rule—

Lick closed a jillion Christmas
   cards,
Sing "Three French Hens" at
   school.

At Grandma's house I ask,
Isn't a Nebraskan Christmas best?
Don't presents, reindeer, and silver
   bulbs

Make a better Christmas than the
   rest?"

Grandma thumbs her Bible,
Reads a manger tale while candles
   flair.
In the dark I barely breathe.
Christmas. Everywhere.
        *—Rochelle Nielsen Barsuhn*

# SANTA IS HERE !

Reindeer prancing through the snow.
Sleigh bells jingling as they go.
Now I know that Santa's near.
This is what I hear:

    Tap, tap, tap!
    Thump, thump, thump!
    Then,
    Down the chimney
    With a bump!

I will not move,
I will not peep!
For Santa thinks
I'm fast asleep!
       *—Jane Belk Moncure*

# THE NIGHT BEFORE CHRISTMAS

*by Clement C. Moore*

'Twas the night before Christmas,
when all through the house
Not a creature was stirring, not
even a mouse;
The stockings were hung by the
chimney with care,
In hopes that St. Nicholas soon
would be there;
The children were nestled all snug
in their beds,
While visions of sugar-plums
danced in their heads;
And mamma in her 'kerchief, and I
in my cap,
Had just settled down for a long
winter's nap,
When out on the lawn there arose
such a clatter,
I sprang from my bed to see what
was the matter.

Away to the window I flew like a
flash,
Tore open the shutters and threw
up the sash.
The moon on the breast of the new-
fallen snow
Gave a lustre of mid-day to
objects below,
When, what to my wondering eyes
should appear,
But a miniature sleigh, and eight
tiny reindeer,
With a little old driver, so lively
and quick,
I knew in a moment it must be St.
Nick.
More rapid than eagles his coursers
they came,
And he whistled, and shouted, and
called them by name:

"Now, Dasher! now, Dancer! now,
Prancer and Vixen!
On, Comet! on, Cupid! on, Donner
and Blitzen!
To the top of the porch! to the top
of the wall!
Now dash away! dash away! dash
away all!"
As dry leaves that before the wild
hurricane fly,
When they meet with an
obstacle, mount to the sky,
So up to the house-top the coursers
they flew,
With a sleigh full of toys, and
St. Nicholas too.
And then, in a twinkling, I heard on
the roof
The prancing and pawing of each
little hoof.
As I drew in my head, and was
turning around,
Down the chimney St. Nicholas
came with a bound.
He was dressed all in fur, from his
head to his foot,
And his clothes were all tarnished
with ashes and soot;
A bundle of toys he had flung on
his back,
And he looked like a peddler just
opening his pack.
His eyes—how they twinkled! his
dimples—how merry!

His cheeks were likes roses,
his nose like a cherry!
His droll little mouth was drawn
up like a bow,
And the beard on his chin was as
white as the snow;
The stump of a pipe he held tight in
his teeth,
And the smoke, it encircled
his head like a wreath;
He had a broad face and a little
round belly
That shook, when he laughed, like
a bowl full of jelly.
He was chubby and plump, a right
jolly old elf,
And I laughed when I saw him, in
spite of myself.
A wink of his eye and a twist of his
head
Soon gave me to know I had
nothing to dread.

He spoke not a word, but went
straight to his work,
And filled all the stockings; then
turned with a jerk,
And laying his finger aside of his
nose
And giving a nod, up the chimney
he rose.

He sprang to his sleigh, to his team
gave a whistle,
And away they all flew like the
down of a thistle.
But I heard him exclaim, as he
drove out of sight,
"Happy Christmas to all, and to all
a good-night."

# IT HAPPENED IN A TOWN CALLED BETHLEHEM

*A BIBLE STORY BASED ON LUKE 2:1-20 AND MATTHEW 2:1-12*
*by Ruth Shannon Odor*

The narrow streets of Bethlehem were crowded with people. People jostled and pushed, some murmuring to each other, others shouting in anger. No one could remember ever before seeing so many people in the tiny town. All these people had come to Bethlehem because of their emperor. He had sent out a decree: all people must go to the home towns of their families to register—so he could tax them!

So it was that a man named Joseph and a woman named Mary came to Bethlehem. Tired from traveling a great distance, they made their way through the great, noisy throng to the inn.

"Have you room?" Joseph asked.

The innkeeper shook his head. "With all these people?" he asked. "There is no room here!" But then he looked beyond Joseph and saw Mary. She would be having a baby soon. And she looked so very, very tired!

"You can stay in the stable," the innkeeper said. "It isn't much, but it's dry."

Joseph turned to Mary. Yes, she nodded. The donkeys and cattle were kept in the stable. At least, it would be quiet.

In the back of the stable, Mary and Joseph made a bed of hay. They went to sleep. The animals slept, too, standing or lying in their stalls. All was quiet and still. The

93

bright stars in the clear night sky shone down on Bethlehem.

Then a wonderful thing happened! Mary gave birth to a baby—God's own Son! Mary wrapped the tiny little baby in strips of cloth and laid Him in a manger for a bed.

Mary and Joseph were not the only people awake that night. Out on a hillside near Bethlehem, some shepherds were taking care of their sheep.

Suddenly a bright light shone around them! An angel stood before them! The shepherds were scared.

"Do not be afraid," said the angel. "I bring you good news—happy news for all people. Tonight the Savior is born in Bethlehem. He is Christ the Lord. You will find the baby wrapped in strips of cloth and lying in a manger."

Suddenly, there were many, many angels! They praised God: "Glory to God in the highest! And on earth, peace among men with whom God is pleased."

As suddenly as they had come, the angels left and went back to Heaven. Once more the night was dark and still. The shepherds could hardly believe what they had seen and heard. A Savior! In Bethlehem! As God had promised!

"Let's go to Bethlehem," they said. "Let's go and see this wonderful thing that has happened!"

The shepherds hurried over the hill to Bethlehem. There they found the stable where Mary and Joseph were. They looked at the tiny baby lying in a manger. This was the Son of God, the Christ.

Then the shepherds told what the angel had said to them. The people of Bethlehem listened and were amazed at this news.

The shepherds left Bethlehem and went back to their sheep. As they walked along, they thanked God and praised Him for all that they had seen and heard.

Later, strange visitors came to the town of Bethlehem. People there were surprised to see them. And the visitors were as surprised as anyone else to be there. In the beginning, they had not known Bethlehem was their destination. They probably had never even

heard of the town. This is how their journey began.

When Jesus was born, Wise-men saw a bright new star in the sky. These Wise-men lived in a land far, far away from Bethlehem, in a land far to the east. They knew that the bright new star was a sign that God's Son, the king of all the world, was born. They had waited for this day.

"We must go and see Him," they said. "It will be a long journey."

"But well worth it. To see God's Son, the king!"

"We'll take gifts."

"Yes, the best gifts we can find!"

So they took gold and frankincense and myrrh, and started out on their long journey to the land of the Jews.

They traveled over hills and mountains, valleys and plains and desert. Day after day after day they traveled.

At last they came to the land of the Jews. Of course they went to the biggest city, Jerusalem. Of course they went to the palace.

Where else would people look for a king?

"Where is He who is born king of the Jews?" they asked. "We saw His star. We have come to worship Him."

The people in the palace did not know anything about a baby king. And King Herod was angry when he heard that these men were looking for a king. After all, *he* was the king.

"In Bethlehem," they said. "The Scriptures say He will be born in Bethlehem."

King Herod held a secret meeting with the Wise-men. He asked them the exact time they had seen the star. Then he said, "Go to Bethlehem. Make a careful search for the Child. As soon as you have found Him, come and tell me. I want to go and worship Him, too."

The Wise-men left Jerusalem and traveled down the road to Bethlehem. And the star that they had seen in the east went ahead of them to show them the way.

The star stopped over one house in Bethlehem. And inside, the

Wise-men found the baby with His mother, Mary.

They looked at Him—this baby who was the Son of God. They knelt before Him and bowed their heads. They thanked God for His Son. Then they opened their treasures and gave Him their gifts.

God knew that King Herod had no intention of worshipping Jesus. In fact, Herod wanted to kill Jesus. So God spoke to the Wise-men in a dream. He told them not to go back to King Herod, and they went back home another way.

As the Wise-men left Bethlehem, they must have looked back with wonder on that tiny town. So this was the place God had chosen as the birthplace of His Son!